Invasive Exotic Plant Monitoring at Tallgrass Priaire National Preserve: Year 1 (2006)

Natural Resource Technical Report NPS/HTLN/NRTR—2007/014
NPS D-31

Craig C. Young, Jennifer L. Haack, J. Tyler Cribbs, and Holly J. Etheridge
National Park Service, Heartland I&M Network
Wilson's Creek National Battlefield, 6424 West Farm Road 182, Republic, MO 65738

Heartland Network

Natural Resource Monitoring

March 2007

U.S. Department of the Interior
National Park Service
Natural Resource Program Center
Fort Collins, Colorado

The Natural Resource Publication series addresses natural resource topics that are of interest and applicability to a broad readership in the National Park Service and to others in the management of natural resources, including the scientific community, the public, and the NPS conservation and environmental constituencies. Manuscripts are peer-reviewed to ensure that the information is scientifically credible, technically accurate, appropriately written for the intended audience, and is designed and published in a professional manner.

The Natural Resource Technical Report series is used to disseminate the peer-reviewed results of scientific studies in the physical, biological, and social sciences for both the advancement of science and the achievement of the National Park Service's mission. The reports provide contributors with a forum for displaying comprehensive data that are often deleted from journals because of page limitations. Current examples of such reports include the results of research that addresses natural resource management issues; natural resource inventory and monitoring activities; resource assessment reports; scientific literature reviews; and peer reviewed proceedings of technical workshops, conferences, or symposia.

Views and conclusions in this report are those of the authors and do not necessarily reflect policies of the National Park Service. Mention of trade names or commercial products does not constitute endorsement or recommendation for use by the National Park Service.

Printed copies of reports in these series may be produced in a limited quantity and they are only available as long as the supply lasts. This report is also available from the Heartland I&M Network website (http://www.nature.nps.gov/im/units/HTLN) on the internet, or by sending a request to the address on the back cover.

Please cite this publication as:

Young, C.C, J.L. Haack, J.T. Cribbs, and H.J. Etheridge. 2007. Invasive exotic plant monitoring at Tallgrass Prairie National Preserve: Year 1 (2006). Natural Resource Technical Report NPS/HTLN/NRTR—2007/014. National Park Service, Fort Collins, Colorado.

NPS D-31, March 2007

Acknowledgements

Dan Tenaglia conducted all field work associated with this report in 2006. Dan died on February 13, 2007 following a collision two days earlier while riding his bike near his home in Opelika, Alabama. We are grateful for his work. Dan's botanical photography can be found at his Missouri Plants website: http://www.missouriplants.com/.

Executive Summary

During surveys in 2006, we documented 16 invasive, exotic plant species on Tallgrass Prairie National Preserve. Six of these exotic plant species were not previously documented as occurring on the park based on NPSpecies, the service-wide database for plant information. Smooth brome, the most abundant invasive plant at Tallgrass Prairie National Preserve, covered between 106 and 226 acres. The grass occurred primarily in improved pasture. Out of the 16 invasive plants, 12 plants occupied less than one acre. In general, invasive, exotic plants are not a major problem at the preserve. The acreage estimates presented in the report may be used to plan management activities leading to control of exotic plants and accomplishment of GPRA goal IA1b.

Table of Contents

This page intentionally left blank.

Introduction

Author's note. In this report, we use the term invasive exotic plant to refer to plants that are not native to the park and that are presumed to pose environmental harm to native plant populations and/or communities based on a review of numerous state and regional invasive exotic plant lists. The great majority of the introductory text was taken from Welch and Geissler (2007) with slight modification.

Scope of invasive exotic plant problem for National Parks. Globalization of commerce, transportation, human migration, and recreation in recent history has introduced invasive exotic species to new areas at an unprecedented rate. Biogeographical barriers that once restricted the location and expansion of species have been circumvented, culminating in the homogenization of the Earth's biota. Although only 10% of introduced species become established and only 1% become problematic (Williamson 1993, Williamson and Fitter 1996) or invasive, nonnative species have profound impacts worldwide on the environment, economies, and human health. Invasive species have been directly linked to the replacement of dominant native species (Tilman 1999), the loss of rare species (King 1985), changes in ecosystem structure, alteration of nutrient cycles and soil chemistry (Ehrenfeld 2003), shifts in community productivity (Vitousek 1990), reduced agricultural productivity, and changes in water availability (D'Antonio and Mahall 1991). Often the damage caused by these species to natural resources is irreparable and our understanding of the consequences incomplete. Invasive species are second only to habitat destruction as a threat to wildland biodiversity (Wilcove et al. 1998). Consequently, the dynamic relationships among plants, animals, soil, and water established over many thousands of years are at risk of being destroyed in a relatively brief period.

For the National Park Service (NPS), the consequences of these invasions present a significant challenge to the management of the agency's natural resources "unimpaired for the enjoyment of future generations." National Parks, like other land management organizations, are deluged by new exotic species arriving through predictable (e.g., road, trail, and riparian corridors), sudden (e.g., long-distance dispersal through cargo containers and air freight), and unexpected anthropogenic pathways (e.g., weed seeds in restoration planting mixes). Nonnative plants claim an estimated 4,600 acres of public lands each year in the United States (Asher and Harmon 1995), significantly altering local flora. For example, exotic plants comprise an estimated 43% and 36% of the flora of the states of Hawaii and New York, respectively (Rejmanek and Randall 1994). Invasive plants infest an estimated 2.6 million acres of the 83 million acres managed by the NPS.

More NPS lands are infested daily despite diligent efforts to curtail the problem. Impacts from invasive species have been realized in most parks, resulting in an expressed need to control existing infestations and restore affected ecosystems. Additionally, there is a growing urgency to be proactive—to protect resources not yet impacted by current and future invasive species (Marler 1998). Invasive exotic species most certainly will continue to be a management priority for the National Parks well into the 21st Century. Invasive exotic plants have been consistently ranked as a top vital sign for long term monitoring as part of the NPS Inventory & Monitoring (I&M) Program. During the vital signs selection process in 2003, Heartland Network parks recognized the need for exotic plant monitoring (DeBacker et al. 2004). Nine parks (CUVA, EFMO, GWCA, HEHO, HOCU, HOME, LIBO, OZAR, PERI) identified invasive exotic plants as their most important management issue, two parks (TAPR, WICR) identified invasive exotic plants as their second most important management issue, and PIPE identified invasive exotic plants as its third most important management issue. During this process, invasive exotic plant monitoring was recognized across all network parks as the most important shared monitoring need.

Prevention and early detection as keys to invasive exotic plant management. Prevention and early detection are the principal strategies for successful invasive exotic plant management. While there is a need for long-term suppression programs to address very high-impact species, eradication efforts are most successful for infestations less than one hectare in size (Rejmanek and Pitcairn 2002). Eradication of infestations larger than 100 hectares is largely unsuccessful, costly, and unsustainable (Rejmanek and Pitcairn 2002). Costs, or impacts, to ecosystem components and processes resulting from invasion also increase dramatically over time, making ecosystem restoration improbable in the later stages of invasion. Further, in their detailed review of the nonnative species problem in the United States, the US Congress, Office of Technology Assessment (1993) stated that the environmental and economic benefits of supporting prevention and early detection initiatives significantly outweigh any incurred costs, with the median benefit-to-cost ratio being 17:1 in favor of being proactive.

Although preventing the introduction of invasive exotic plants is the most successful and preferred strategy for resource managers, the realities of globalization, tight fiscal constraints, and limited staff time guarantee that invaders will get through park borders. Fortunately, invasive exotic plants quite often undergo a lag period between introduction and subsequent colonization of new areas. Managers, then, can take advantage of early detection monitoring to make certain invasive exotic species are found and successfully eradicated before populations become well established.

This strategy requires resource managers to: (1) detect invasive exotic species early (i.e., find a new species or an incipient population of an existing species while the infestation is small (less than 1 hectare), and (2) respond rapidly (i.e., implement appropriate management techniques to eliminate the invasive plant and all of its associated regenerative material).

Invasive exotic plant management at Tallgrass Prairie National Preseve. While a complete history of park invasive exotic plant management issues is beyond the scope of this report, a few important highlights are given:

1. Sericea lespedeza (*Lespedeza cuneata*) was documented at Tallgrass Prairie in 2006. The invasion was relatively small.

2. Caucasian bluestem (*Bothriochloa bladhii*) was planted to control erosion and is known from pond dams and developed areas at the park.

3. The park is restoring a large field on the eastern side of the park that was planted in smooth brome (*Bromus inermis*).

4. Disturbance associated with roads, trails, and, possibly, cattle feeding areas may facilitate the invasion of exotic plants.

Methods

Watch lists. The invasive exotic plants on three watch lists were sought during monitoring (Table 1). Invasive exotic plants not known to occur on the park based on NPSpecies (the national NPS database for plant occurrence registration) constitute the early detection watch list. Invasive exotic plants known to occur on the park based on NPSpecies constitute the park-established watch list. Invasive exotic plants from the park-based watch list included plants selected by park managers or network staff which may not have been included on the other lists due to incomplete information in NPSpecies (e.g., not documented) or USDA Plants (e.g., state distribution information inaccurate) databases or due to differing opinions regarding network designation of a plant as a high priority. While aquatic species are listed on the watch lists, terrestrial plants were the focus of this survey. Aquatic plants were documented occasionally.

Field methods. Invasive exotic plant species on designated watch lists (Table 1) were sought in high priority areas on Tallgrass Prairie National Preserve (Figure 1). Dan Tenaglia, the contract botanist for this project, used a Thales GPS unit to navigate along 400 m line transects, identified invasive exotic plants in an approximately 6-m belt, and attributed a coarse cover value to each species (0=0, 1=0.1-0.9 m^2, 2=1-9.9 m^2, 3=10-49.9 m^2, 4= 50-99.9 m^2, 5=100-499.9 m^2, 6= 499.9-999.9 m^2, 7=1000-4999.9 m^2, 8=5000-9999.9 m^2, and 9=10,000-14999.9 m^2). A total of 301 transects were surveyed at Tallgrass Prairie National Preserve. Of these, 274 transects were 400 m in length, while 27 were clipped by the park boundary. The observer had discretion to search a larger belt if feasible, to search additional areas up to a 200 m perpendicular distance from the transect, to target locations likely to support exotic plants (e.g., field edges, roads), and to circumvent extremely difficult or hazardous terrain when needed. However, in most cases, the observer maintained the established line transect. Cover was estimated for all plants observed while navigating along the transect (i.e., not restricted to the 6-m belt).

Analytical methods. Data analysis involved simple displays, as well as calculation of plant frequency and cover. The invasive exotic plants encountered on Tallgrass Prairie National Preserve were attributed to line transects in a GIS. Polygons surrounding occupied line transects were highlighted on maps for each invasive exotic plant encountered (Figures 3 – 18). Note that entire polygons were not fully searched. The park-wide frequency of invasive exotic plants was calculated as the percentage of occupied transects. A park-wide cover range was estimated using the high and low values of the cover classes for each invasive exotic plant encountered, assuming that 3 % of the park was searched and that the areas searched were representative of the entire park. As a check on our estimates, we also estimated the extent of smooth brome (*Bromus inermis*) with a mapping approach (Figure 2). Because smooth brome is largely restricted to improved pastures at Tallgrass Prairie National Preserve, mapping these pastures provided a relatively accurate estimate of its extent.

Invasiveness ranks. In order to provide additional information on the ecological impact and feasibility of control, the ecological impact and general management difficulty sub-ranks that constitute the invasiveness rank (I-rank), as determined by NatureServe (Morse et al. 2004), were listed when available. The ecological impact characterizes the effect of the plant on ecosystem processes, community composition and structure, native plant and animal populations, and the conservation significance of threatened biodiversity. General management difficulty ranks are assigned based on the resources and time generally required to control a plant, the non-target effects of control on native populations, and the accessibility of invaded sites. Sub-ranks are given as high (H), medium (M), low (L), insignificant (I), unknown (U), or a combination of ranks.

Results and Discussion

In 2006, a total of 16 invasive exotic plant taxa were found during the survey at Tallgrass Prairie National Preserve (Table 2). Of these plants, seven taxa were known to occur on the park based on the NPSpecies database. Three plants not designated as high priority species by the network were added to the watch list based on the survey: bald brome (*Bromus racemosus*), buffalobur nightshade (*Solanum rostratum*), and the invasive native eastern redcedar (*Juniperus virginiana*). The species identified on the early detection list will be entered in NPSpecies and should subsequently be included on the park-established watch list.

The distribution and abundance of the invasive exotic plant species at Tallgrass Prairie National Preserve varied widely. One species was moderately widespread and abundant with cover between 106 and 226 acres: smooth brome. However, smooth brome (*Bromus inermis*) was restricted to or near areas where the grass was intentionally planted. Bald brome was more widespread, but only occupied between five and 28 acres on the park. The most widely distributed exotic plant, buffalobur nightshade, only occupied less than three acres and is weedy, but not highly invasive. Johnsongrass (*Sorghum halepense*) was moderately widespread and abundant, occurring primarily in improved pasture. Twelve species occupied less than one acre and were encountered with a relatively low frequency.

After mapping the improved pastures (Figure 2), we estimated that smooth brome dominated 518 acres on Tallgrass Prairie National Preserve. This estimate most accurately characterizes the extent of smooth brome on the preserve, especially for the purposes of restoration planning. The variance of this estimate with the sampling estimate of 106 to 226 acres suggests that the sampling estimate may be off by some factor. This difference likely arises from a combination of sampling error, measurement error, and scaling error. The difference may also reflect a difference in definitions: the sampling approach tries to estimate only the area covered by smooth brome within pastures.

No species were noted as having unambiguously high ecological impact. Narrowleaf cattail (*Typha angustifolia*) and black locust (*Robinia pseudoacacia*) may have a high ecological impact (Table 2). Seven species were characterized as having a medium or medium-low ecological impact. Johnsongrass and spotted knapweed were noted as being potentially difficult to manage, while management difficulty was medium or less for the remaining species.

In summary, this report provides information on invasive, exotic plant abundance and distribution as well as ecological impacts and management difficulty to assist park natural resource managers in planning invasive exotic plant management. The following links may further assist managers: http://www.nature.nps.gov/im/units/htln/monitoring/projects/inp.htm and http://www.natureserve.org/explorer/.

Literature Cited

Asher, J. A., and D. W. Harmon. 1995. Invasive exotic plants are destroying the naturalness of U.S. Wilderness areas. International Journal of Wilderness 1:35-37.

D'Antonio, C. M., and B. E. Mahall. 1991. Root profiles and competition between the invasive, exotic perennial, *Carpobrotus edulis,* and two native shrub species in California coastal scrub. American Journal of Botany 78:885-894.

DeBacker, M.D., C.C. Young (editor), P. Adams, L. Morrison, D. Peitz, G.A. Rowell, M. Williams, and D. Bowles. 2005. Heartland Inventory and Monitoring Network and Prairie Cluster Prototype Monitoring Program Vital Signs Monitoring Plan. National Park Service, Heartland Inventory and Monitoring Network and Prairie Cluster Prototype Monitoring Program, Wilson's Creek National Battlefield, Republic, Missouri, 104 pp. plus appendices.

Ehrenfeld, J.G. 2003. The effects of exotic plant invasions on soil nutrient cycling processes. Ecosystems 6:503-523.

King, W. B. 1985. Island birds: will the future repeat the past? Pages 3-15 *in* P. J. Moors, editor. Conservation of Island Birds. International Council for Bird Preservation. Cambridge University Press, Cambridge, UK.

Marler, M. 1998. Exotic plant invasions of federal Wilderness areas: current status and future directions. The Aldo Leopold Wilderness Research Institute. Rocky Mountain Research Station, Missoula, Montana, USA.

Office of Technology Assessment. 1993. Harmful non-indigenous species in the United States. OTA-F-565. U.S. Congress, Government Printing Office, Washington, D.C., USA.

Rejmanek, M., and M. J. Pitcairn. 2002. When is eradication of exotic pest plants a realistic goal? Pages 249-253 in C. R. Veitch and M. N. Clout, editors. Turning the Tide: the Eradication of Invasive Species. IUCN SSC Invasive Species Specialist Group. IUCN, Gland, Switzerland and Cambridge, UK.

Rejmanek, M., and J. M. Randall. 1994. Invasive alien plants in California: 1993 summary and comparison with other areas in North America. Madrono 41:161–177.

Tilman, D. 1999. The ecological consequences of changes in biodiversity: a search for general principles. Ecology 80:1455-1474.

Vitousek, P. M. 1990. Biological invasions and ecosystem processes: towards an integration of population biology and ecosystem studies. Oikos 57:7-13.

Welch, B.A. and P.H. Geissler. 2007. Early detection of invasive plants: a handbook. United States Geological Survey draft. http://www.pwrc.usgs.gov/brd/invasiveHandbook.cfm.

Wilcove, D. S., D. Rothstein, J. Dubow, A. Phillips, and E. Losos. 1998. Quantifying threats to imperiled species in the United States. Bioscience 48:607–615.

Williamson, M. 1993. Invaders, weeds and risk from genetically modified organisms. Experientia 49:219–224.

Williamson, M. and A. Fitter. 1996. The varying success of invaders. Ecology 77:1661–1666.

Tallgrass Prairie National Preserve
Exotic Plant Search Line Transects

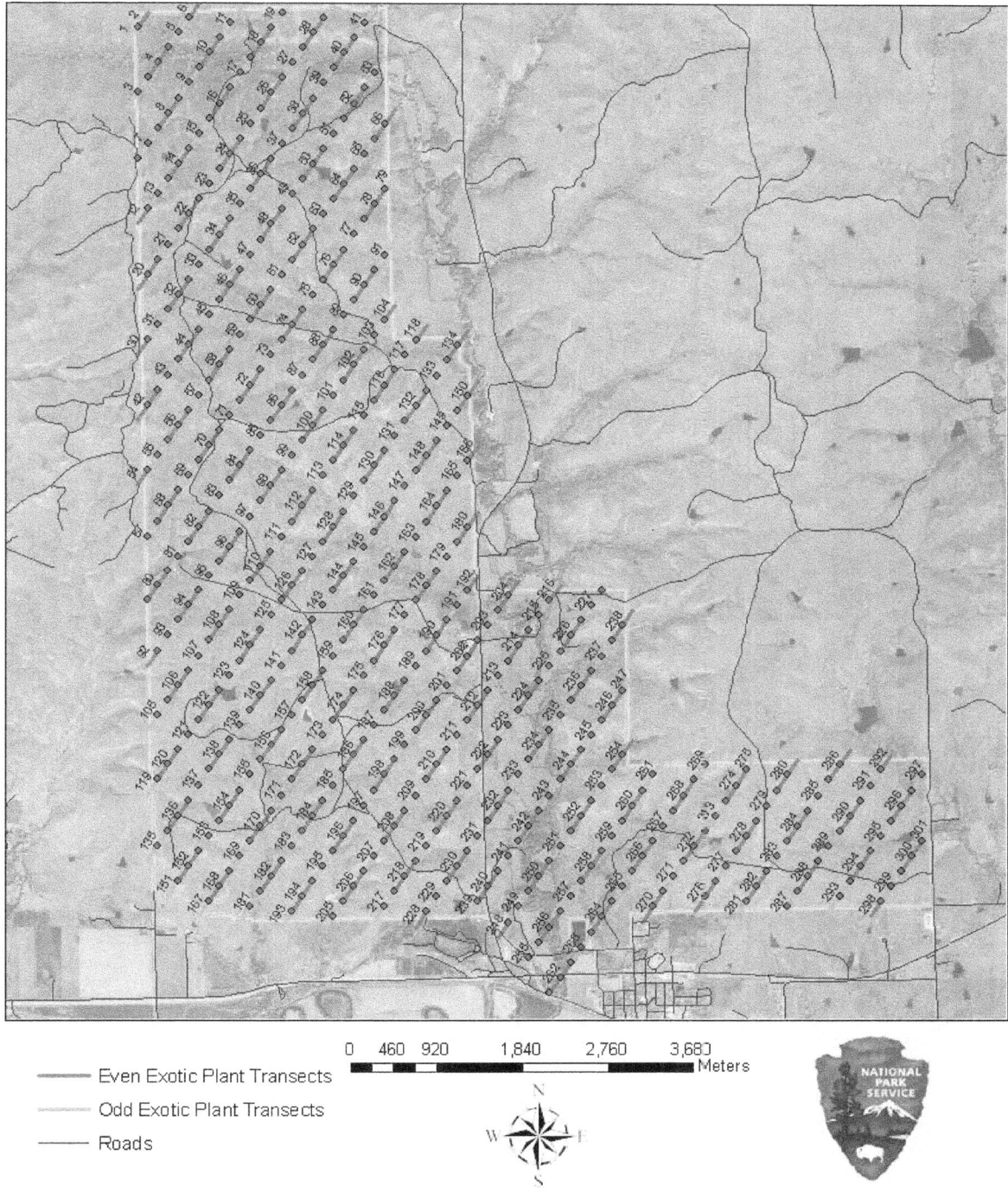

	0	460	920	1,840	2,760	3,680

Meters

——— Even Exotic Plant Transects

——— Odd Exotic Plant Transects

——— Roads

Figure 1. Invasive exotic plant line transects at Tallgrass Prairie National Preserve. The blue (even numbered) and orange (odd numbered) transects indicate the search locations for invasive exotic plants in 2006.

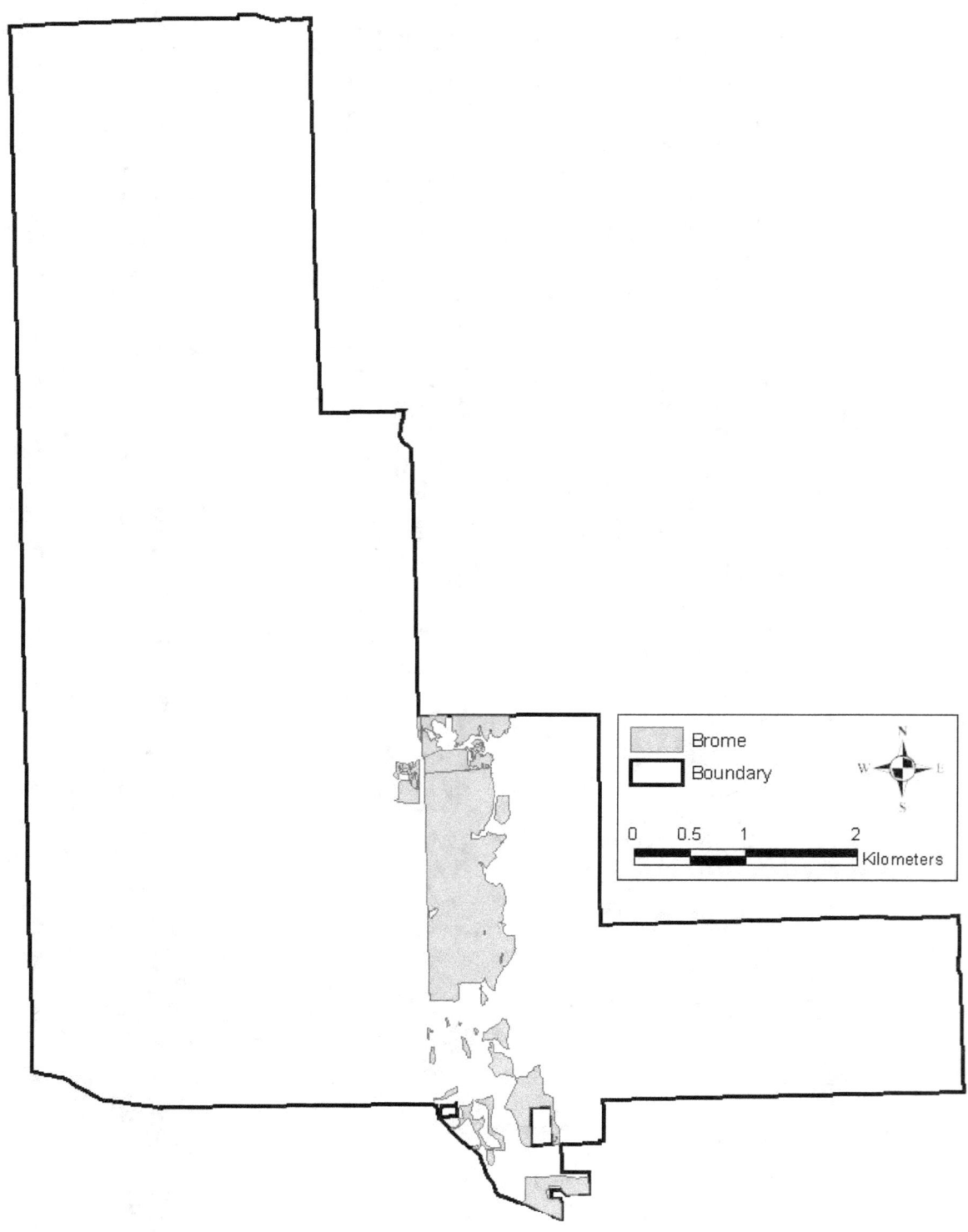

Figure 2.Smooth brome (*Bromus inermis*) locations at Tallgrass Prairie National Preserve. Total acreage of smooth brome is estimated as 518 acres.

Table 1. Watch lists for Tallgrass Prairie National Preserve

Early Detection Watch List		Park-Established Watch List		Park-Based Watch List	
Ailanthus altissima	Tree of heaven	Alliaria petiolata	Garlic mustard	Bassia scoparia	Burningbush
Alnus glutinosa	European alder	Arctium minus	Lesser burdock	Bromus racemosus	Bald brome
Arundo donax	Giant reed	Bromus inermis	Smooth brome	Cirsium arvense	Canada thistle
Azolla	Mosquitofern	Bromus tectorum	Cheatgrass	Juniperus virginiana	Eastern redcedar
Berberis thunbergii	Japanese barberry	Carduus nutans	Nodding plumeless thistle	Solanum rostratum	Buffalobur nightshade
Bothriochloa bladhii	Caucasian bluestem	Holcus lanatus	Common velvetgrass		
Centaurea solstitialis	Yellow star-thistle	Melilotus officinalis	Yellow sweetclover		
Centaurea stoebe ssp. micranthos	Spotted knapweed	Morus alba	White mulberry		
Cirsium vulgare	Bull thistle	Poa pratensis	Kentucky bluegrass		
Cynanchum louiseae	Louise's swallow-wort	Robinia pseudoacacia	Black locust		
Dactylis glomerata	Orchardgrass	Rosa multiflora	Multiflora rose		
Dioscorea oppositifolia	Chinese yam	Sorghum halepense	Johnsongrass		
Dipsacus fullonum	Fuller's teasel	Ulmus pumila	Siberian elm		
Dipsacus laciniatus	Cutleaf teasel	Verbascum thapsus	Common mullein		
Egeria densa	Brazilian waterweed				
Elaeagnus angustifolia	Russian olive				
Elaeagnus umbellata	Autumn olive				
Euonymus fortunei	Winter creeper				
Euphorbia esula	Leafy spurge				
Glechoma hederacea	Ground ivy				
Hesperis matronalis	Dames rocket				
Humulus japonicus	Japanese hop				
Lespedeza bicolor	Shrub lespedeza				
Lespedeza cuneata	Sericea lespedeza				
Lonicera japonica	Japanese honeysuckle				
Lonicera maackii	Amur honeysuckle				
Lonicera tatarica	Tatarian honeysuckle				
Lotus corniculatus	Bird's-foot trefoil				
Lotus glaber	Narrow-leaf bird's-foot trefoil				
Lysimachia nummularia	Creeping jenny				

Table 1. Watch lists for Tallgrass Prairie National Preserve (cont.)

Early Detection Watch List		Park-Established Watch List	Park-Based Watch List
Lythrum salicaria	Purple loosestrife		
Myriophyllum aquaticum	Parrot feather watermilfoil		
Pastinaca sativa	Wild parsnip		
Phalaris arundinacea	Reed canarygrass		
Phragmites australis	Common reed		
Plantago lanceolata	Narrowleaf plantain		
Poa compressa	Canada bluegrass		
Polygonum cuspidatum	Japanese knotweed		
Populus alba	White poplar		
Potamogeton crispus	Curly pondweed		
Potentilla recta	Sulphur cinquefoil		
Pueraria montana var. lobata	Kudzu		
Pyrus calleryana	Callery pear		
Rhamnus cathartica	Common buckthorn		
Schedonorus phoenix	Tall fescue		
Schedonorus pratensis	Meadow fescue		
Securigera varia	Crownvetch		
Solanum dulcamara	Climbing nightshade		
Tamarix ramosissima	Saltcedar		
Torilis arvensis	Spreading hedgeparsley		
Torilis japonica	Erect hedgeparsley		
Typha angustifolia	Narrowleaf cattail		
Vinca minor	Common periwinkle		

Table 2. Overview of invasive exotic plants found on Tallgrass Prairie National Preserve. Ecological impact and general management difficulty based on NatureServe I-Rank subranks, Morse et al. 2004. Subranks are given as high (H), medium (M), low (L), insignificant (I), unknown (U), a range of ranks (indicated by /), or not available (--).

Scientific Name	Common Name	Watch list	Park-wide cover (acres)	Frequency (percent)	Ecological impact	Management difficulty
Bromus inermis	Smooth brome	Park-established	106.2 – 225.5	7.0	M	ML
Bromus racemosus	Bald brome	Add to park-based	11.6 – 56.2	14.0	--	--
Sorghum halepense	Johnson grass	Park-established	0.9 – 3.7	4.0	ML	HM
Solanum rostratum	Buffalobur nightshade	Add to park-based	0.3 – 2.9	22.6	--	--
Schedonorus spp.	Fescue species	Add to park-based	< 1.0	1.0	--	--
Alliaria petiolata	Garlic mustard	Park-established	< 0.75	1.7	ML	M
Robinia pseudoacacia	Black locust	Park-established	< 0.5	0.3	HM	M
Juniperus virginiana	Eastern redcedar	Park-based	< 0.5	2.3	--	--
Morus alba	White mulberry	Park-established	< 0.5	1.0	ML	ML
Pyrus calleryana	Callery pear	Early detection	< 0.5	0.3	LI	ML
Torilis japonica	Erect hedgeparsley	Early detection	< 0.5	2.3	--	--
Typha angustifolia	Narrowleaf cattail	Early detection	< 0.25	1.0	HM	M
Cirsium vulgare	Bull thistle	Early detection	< 0.25	1.0	ML	ML
Melilotus officinalis	Sweetclover	Park-established	< 0.1	0.7	M	M
Arctium minus	Lesser burdock	Park-established	< 0.1	1.0	LI	MI
Centaurea stoebe ssp. micranthos	Spotted knapweed	Early detection	< 0.01	0.3	M	HL

Figure 3. Abundance and distribution of *Alliaria petiolata* (garlic-mustard) at Tallgrass Prairie National Preserve, 2006. Cover classes are as follows: 1=0.1-0.9 m^2, 2=1-9.9 m^2, 3=10-49.9 m^2, 4= 50-99.9 m^2, 5=100-499.9 m^2, 6= 499.9-999.9 m^2, 7=1,000-4,999.9 m^2, 8=5,000-9,999.9 m^2, and 9=10,000-14,999.9.

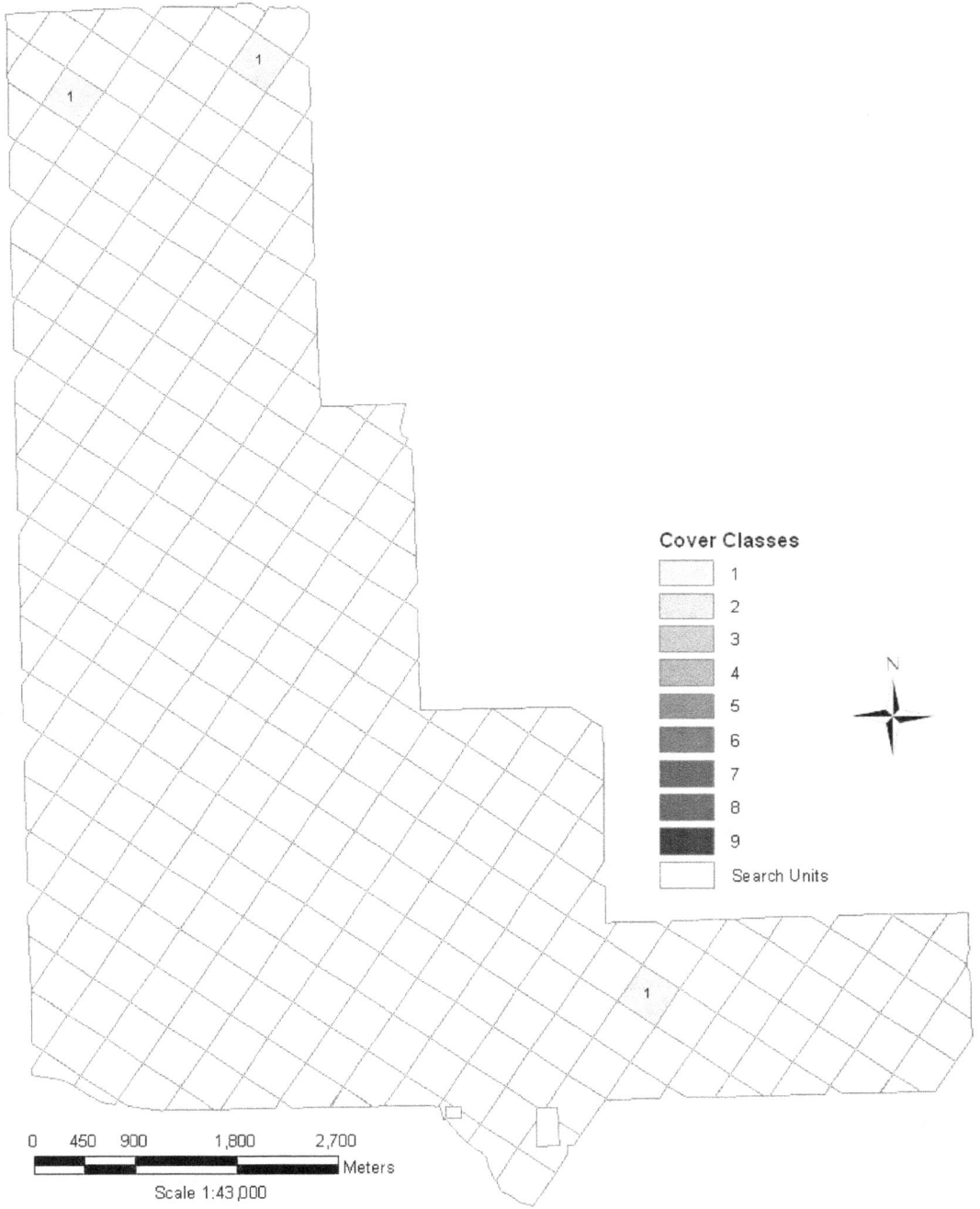

Figure 4. Abundance and distribution of *Arctium minus* (lesser burdock) at Tallgrass Prairie National Preserve, 2006. Cover classes are as follows: 1=0.1-0.9 m², 2=1-9.9 m², 3=10-49.9 m², 4= 50-99.9 m², 5=100-499.9 m², 6= 499.9-999.9 m², 7=1,000-4,999.9 m², 8=5,000-9,999.9 m², and 9=10,000-14,999.9.

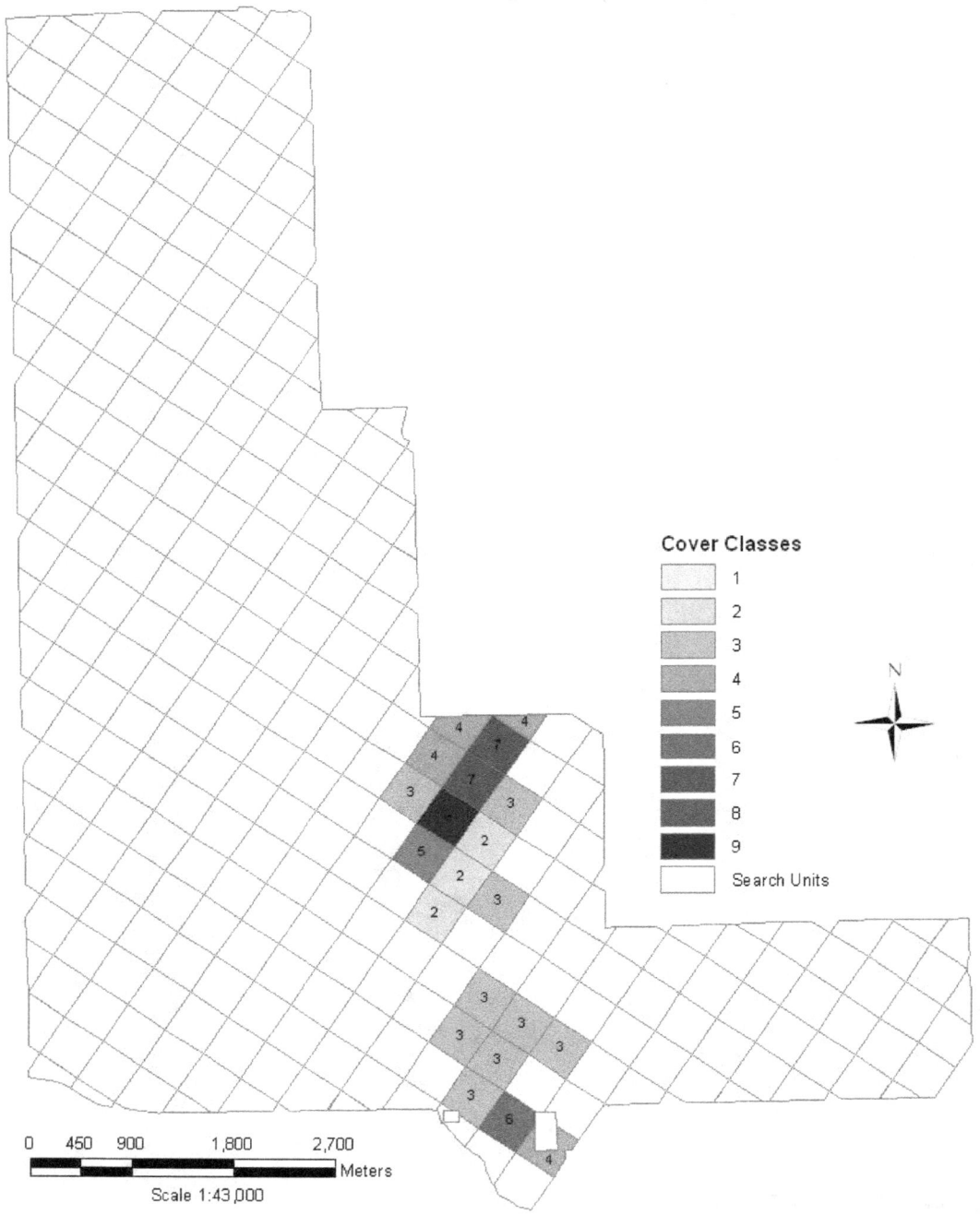

Figure 5. Abundance and distribution of *Bromus inermis* (smooth brome) at Tallgrass Prairie National Preserve, 2006. Cover classes are as follows: 1=0.1-0.9 m^2, 2=1-9.9 m^2, 3=10-49.9 m^2, 4= 50-99.9 m^2, 5=100-499.9 m^2, 6= 499.9-999.9 m^2, 7=1,000-4,999.9 m^2, 8=5,000-9,999.9 m^2, and 9=10,000-14,999.9.

Bromus racemosus - 2006

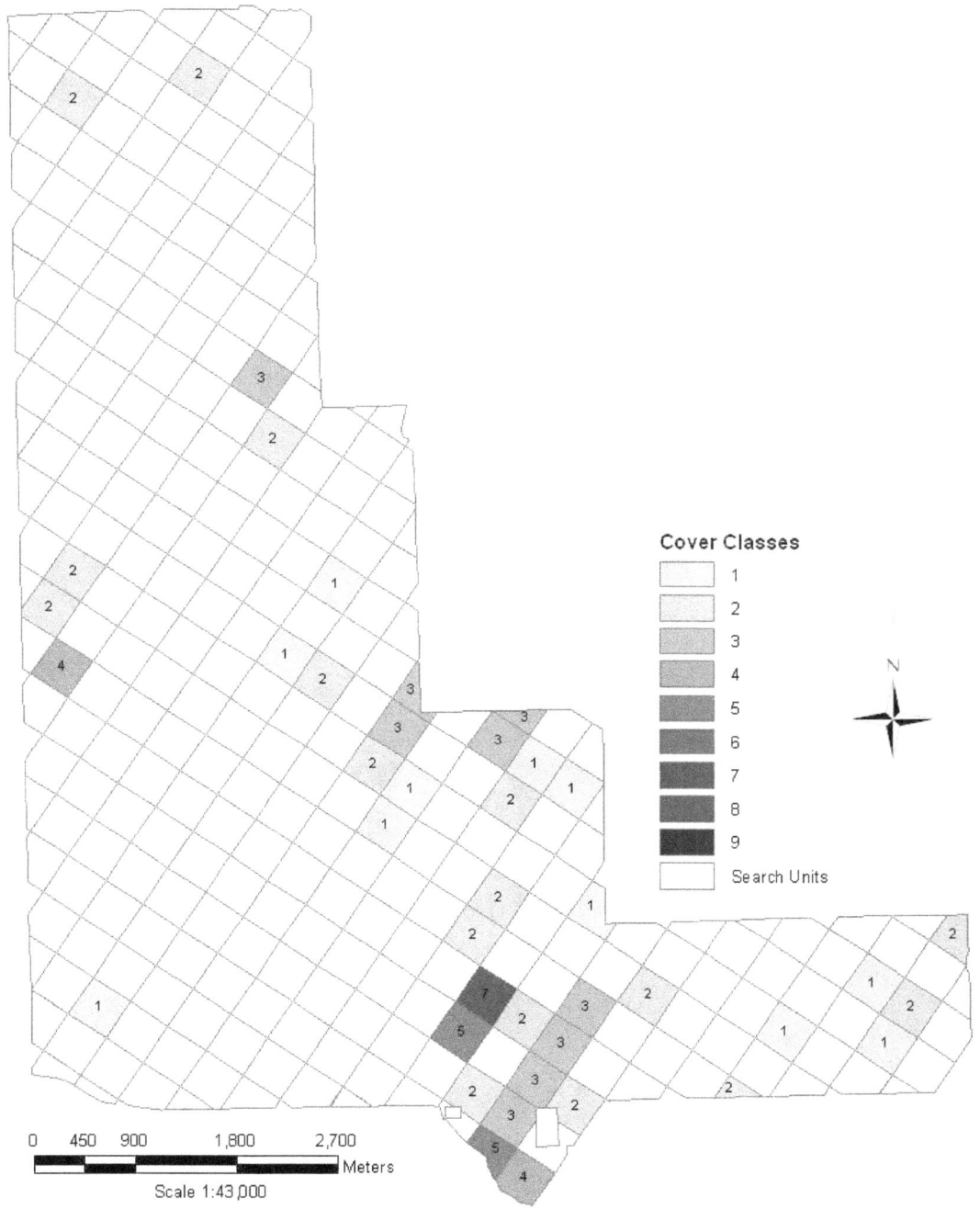

Figure 6. Abundance and distribution of *Bromus racemosus* (bald brome) at Tallgrass Prairie National Preserve, 2006. Cover classes are as follows: 1=0.1-0.9 m², 2=1-9.9 m², 3=10-49.9 m², 4= 50-99.9 m², 5=100-499.9 m², 6= 499.9-999.9 m², 7=1,000-4,999.9 m², 8=5,000-9,999.9 m², and 9=10,000-14,999.9.

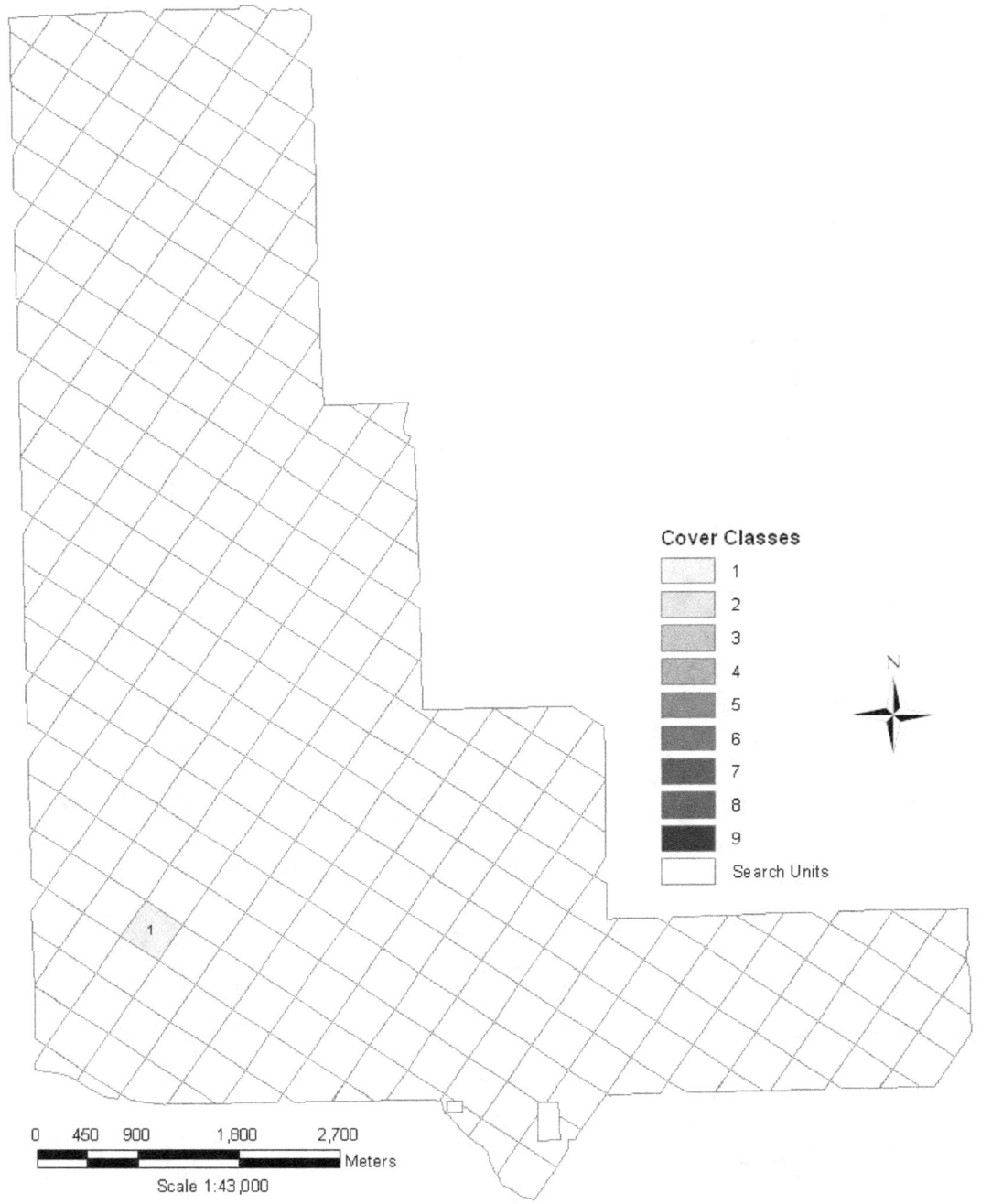

Centaurea stoebe ssp micranthos - 2006

Cover Classes

	1
	2
	3
	4
	5
	6
	7
	8
	9
	Search Units

0   450   900   1,800   2,700
Meters
Scale 1:43,000

Figure 7. Abundance and distribution of *Centaurea stoebe ssp. micranthos* (spotted knapweed) at Tallgrass Prairie National Preserve, 2006. Cover classes are as follows: 1=0.1-0.9 m², 2=1-9.9 m², 3=10-49.9 m², 4= 50-99.9 m², 5=100-499.9 m², 6= 499.9-999.9 m², 7=1,000-4,999.9 m², 8=5,000-9,999.9 m², and 9=10,000-14,999.9.

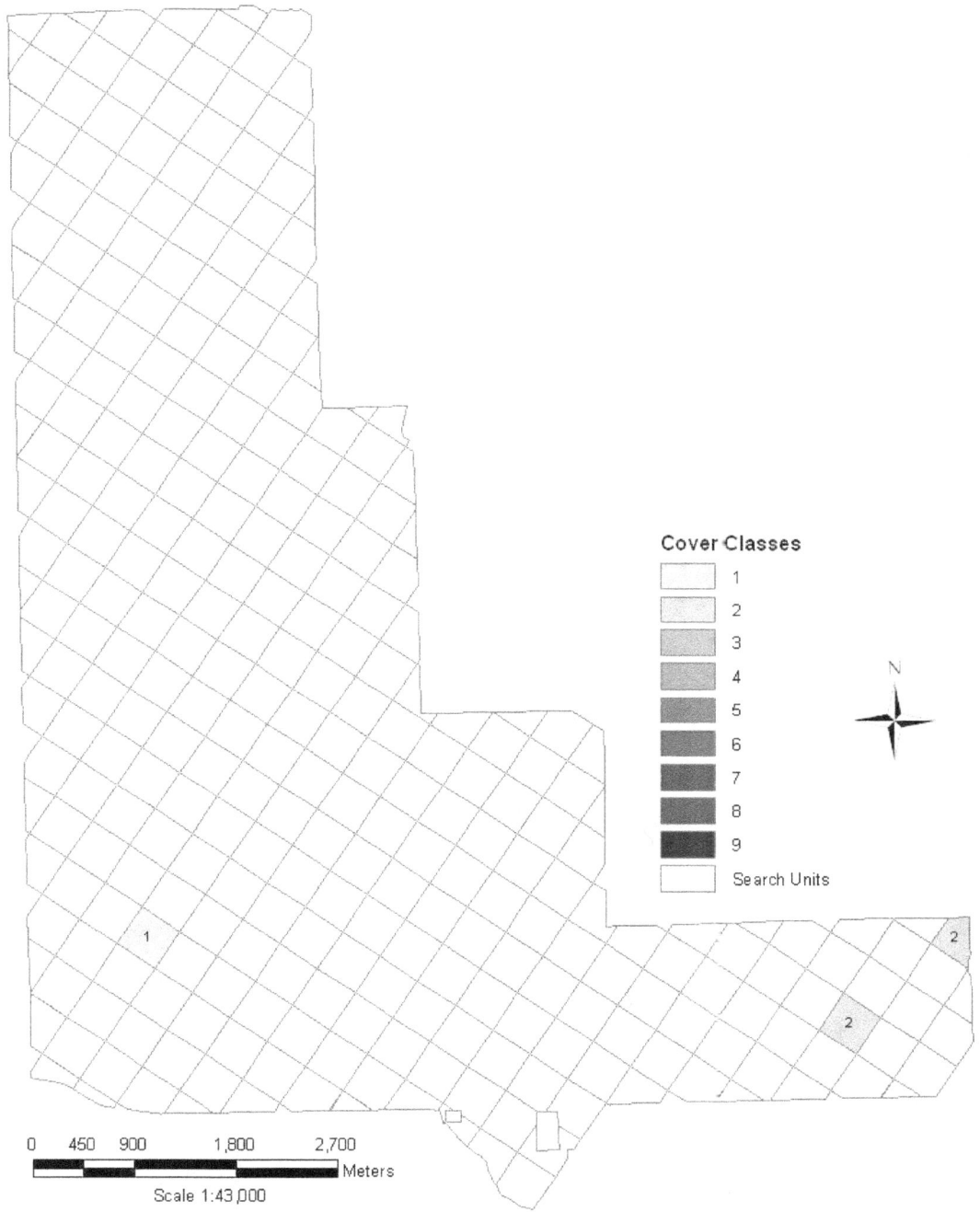

Figure 8. **Abundance and distribution of *Cirsium vulgare* (bull thistle) at Tallgrass Prairie National Preserve, 2006. Cover classes are as follows: 1=0.1-0.9 m^2, 2=1-9.9 m^2, 3=10-49.9 m^2, 4= 50-99.9 m^2, 5=100-499.9 m^2, 6= 499.9-999.9 m^2, 7=1,000-4,999.9 m^2, 8=5,000-9,999.9 m^2, and 9=10,000-14,999.9.**

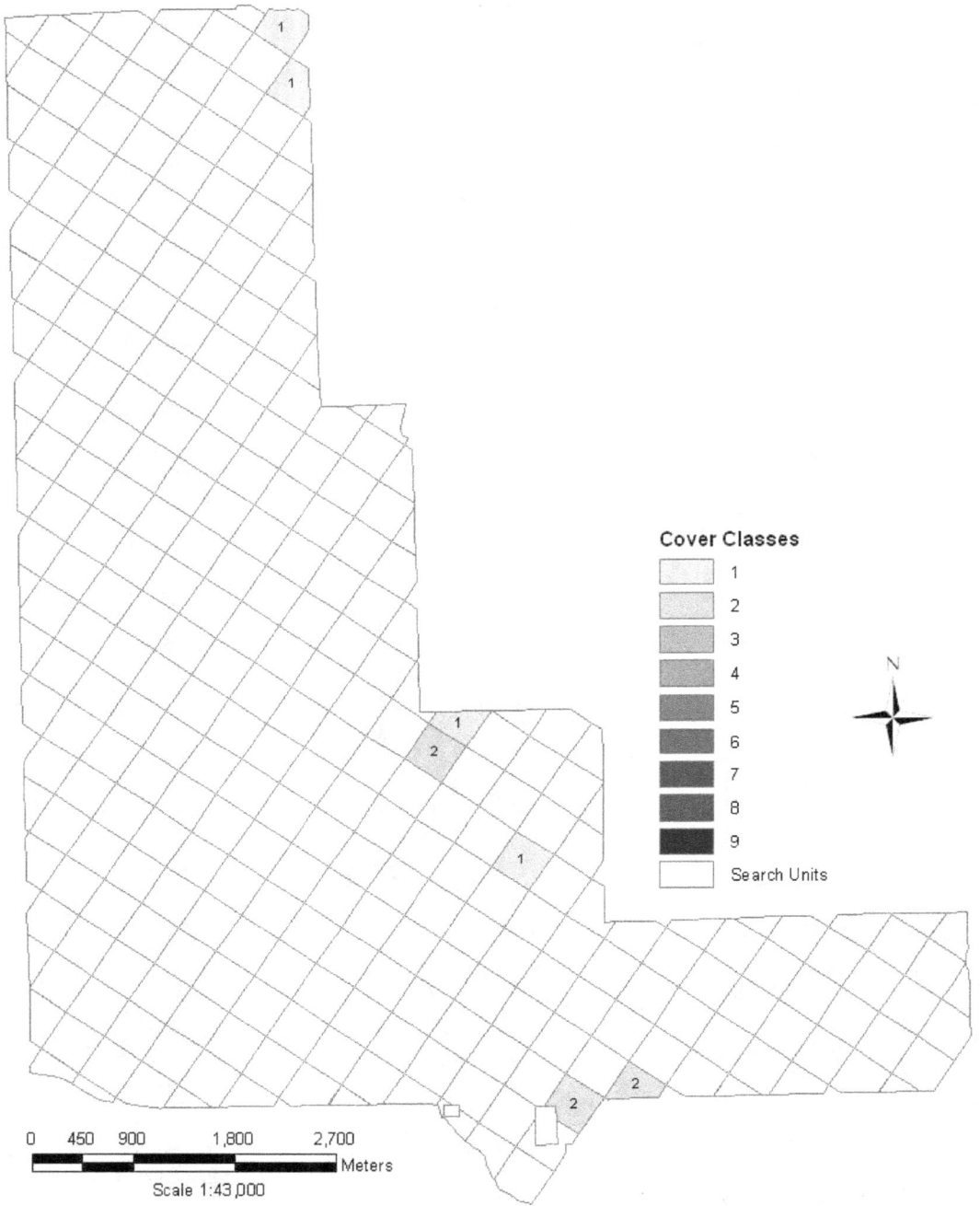

Juniperus virginiana - 2006

Cover Classes

1
2
3
4
5
6
7
8
9
Search Units

0 450 900   1,800   2,700
                                    Meters
Scale 1:43,000

Figure 9. Abundance and distribution of *Juniperus virginiana* (Eastern redcedar) at Tallgrass Prairie National Preserve, 2006. Cover classes are as follows: 1=0.1-0.9 m², 2=1-9.9 m², 3=10-49.9 m², 4= 50-99.9 m², 5=100-499.9 m², 6= 499.9-999.9 m², 7=1,000-4,999.9 m², 8=5,000-9,999.9 m², and 9=10,000-14,999.9.

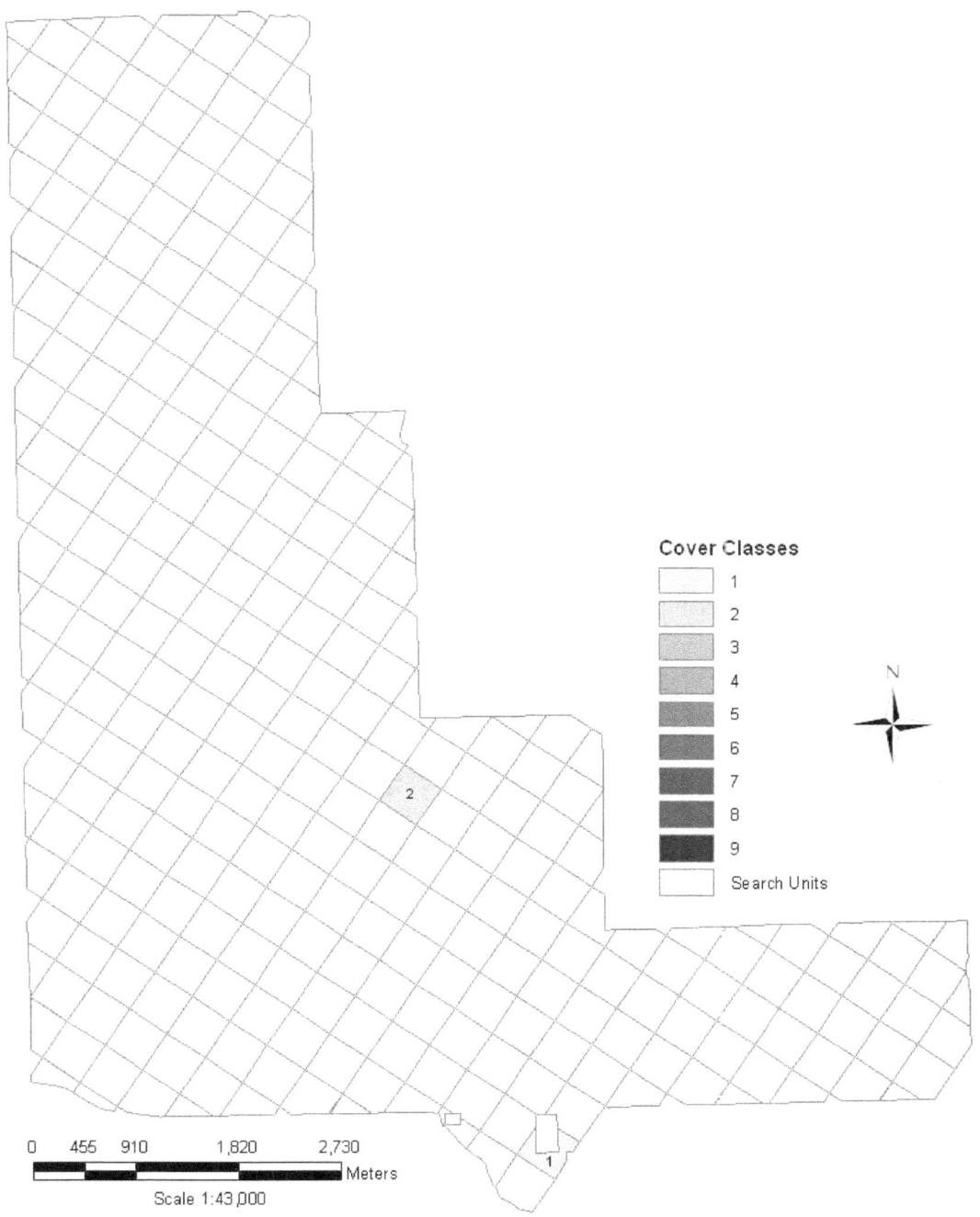

Figure 10. Abundance and distribution of *Melilotus officinalis* (yellow sweet clover) at Tallgrass Prairie National Preserve, 2006. Cover classes are as follows: 1=0.1-0.9 m², 2=1-9.9 m², 3=10-49.9 m², 4= 50-99.9 m², 5=100-499.9 m², 6= 499.9-999.9 m², 7=1,000-4,999.9 m², 8=5,000-9,999.9 m², and 9=10,000-14,999.9.

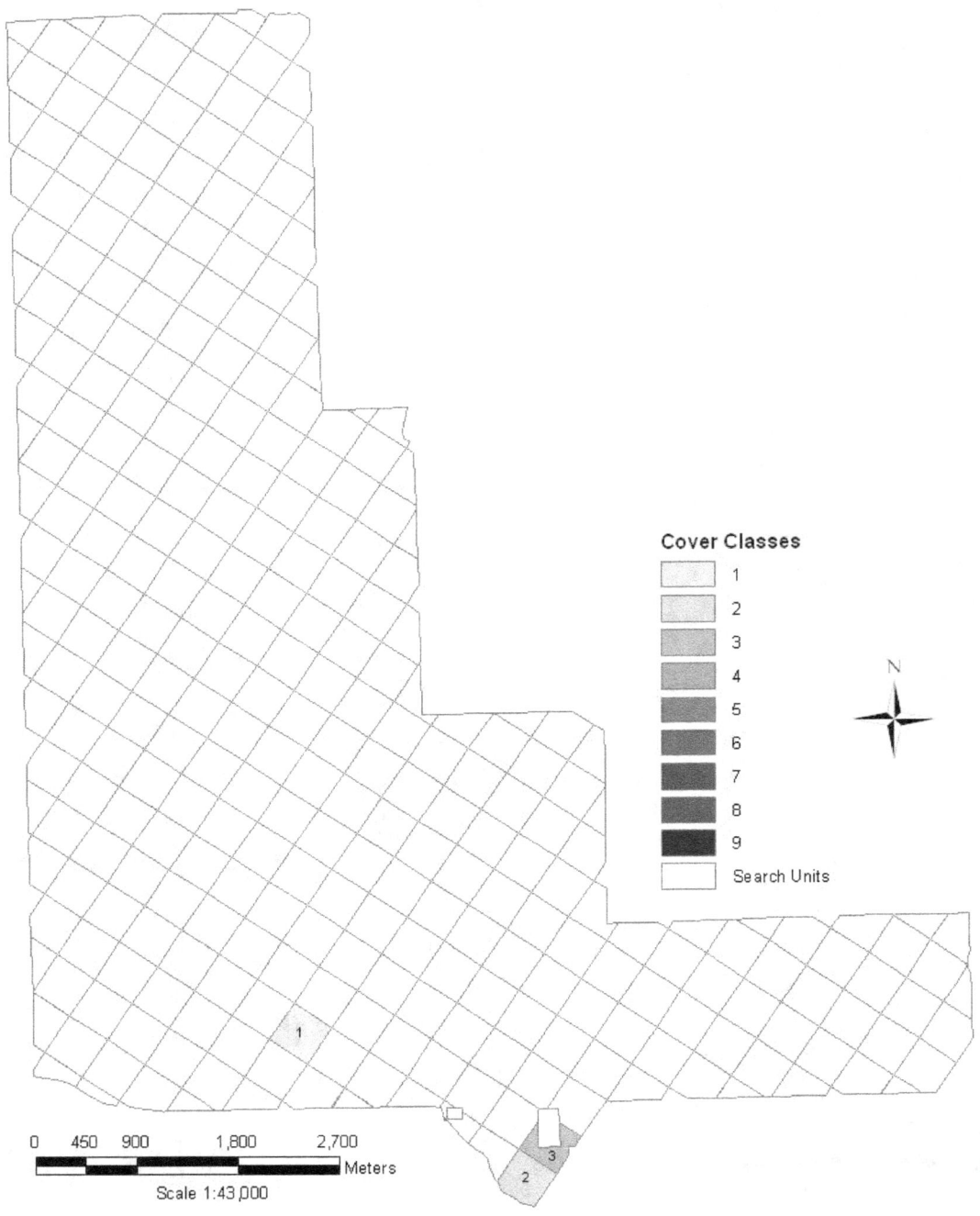

Figure 11. Abundance and distribution of *Morus alba* (white mulberry) at Tallgrass Prairie National Preserve, 2006. Cover classes are as follows: 1=0.1-0.9 m^2, 2=1-9.9 m^2, 3=10-49.9 m^2, 4= 50-99.9 m^2, 5=100-499.9 m^2, 6= 499.9-999.9 m^2, 7=1,000-4,999.9 m^2, 8=5,000-9,999.9 m^2, and 9=10,000-14,999.9.

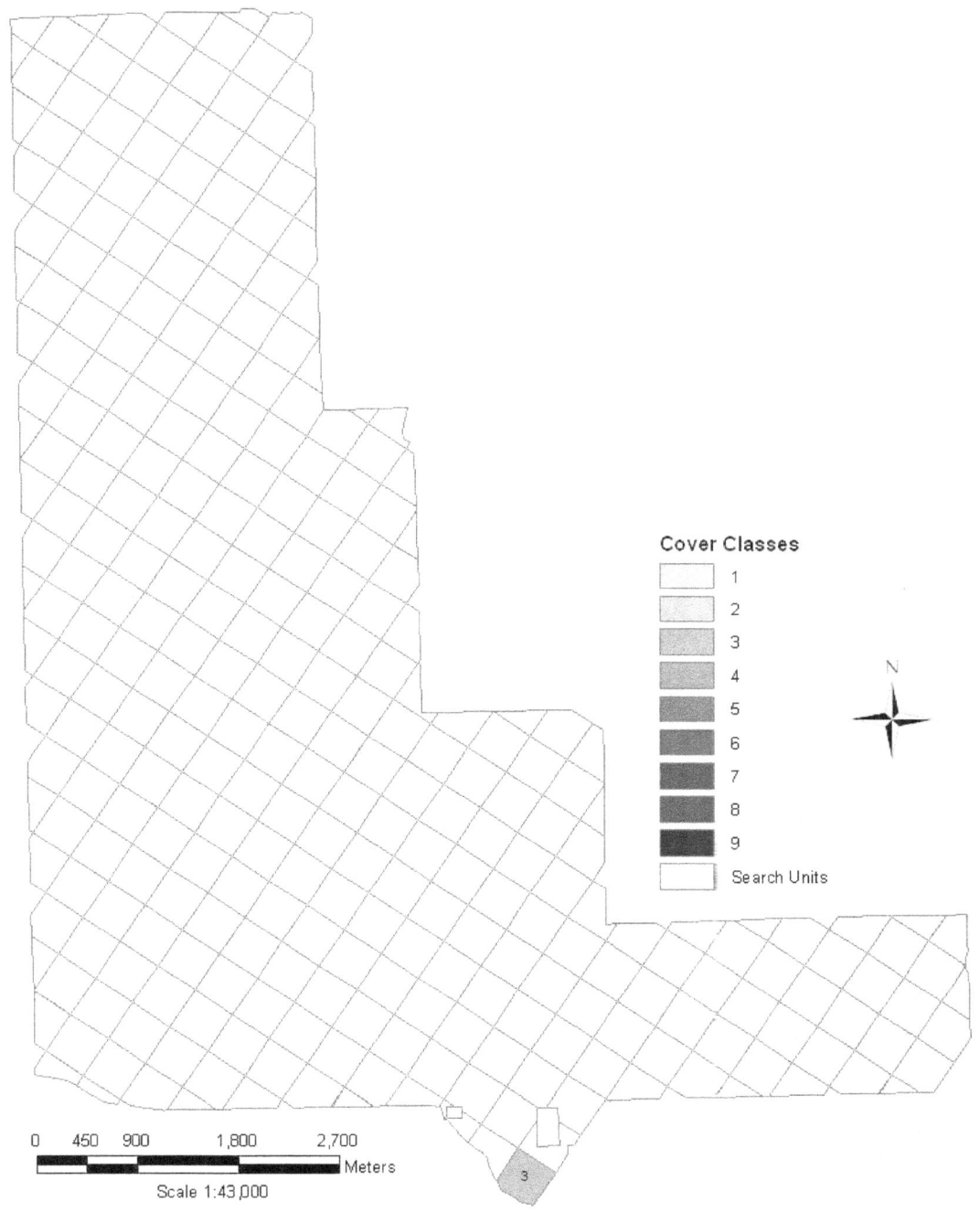

Pyrus calleryana - 2006

Cover Classes

1
2
3
4
5
6
7
8
9

Search Units

0   450   900   1,800   2,700
Meters
Scale 1:43,000

Figure 12. Abundance and distribution of *Pyrus calleryana* (callery pear) at Tallgrass Prairie National Preserve, 2006. Cover classes are as follows: 1=0.1-0.9 m^2, 2=1-9.9 m^2, 3=10-49.9 m^2, 4= 50-99.9 m^2, 5=100-499.9 m^2, 6= 499.9-999.9 m^2, 7=1,000-4,999.9 m^2, 8=5,000-9,999.9 m^2, and 9=10,000-14,999.9.

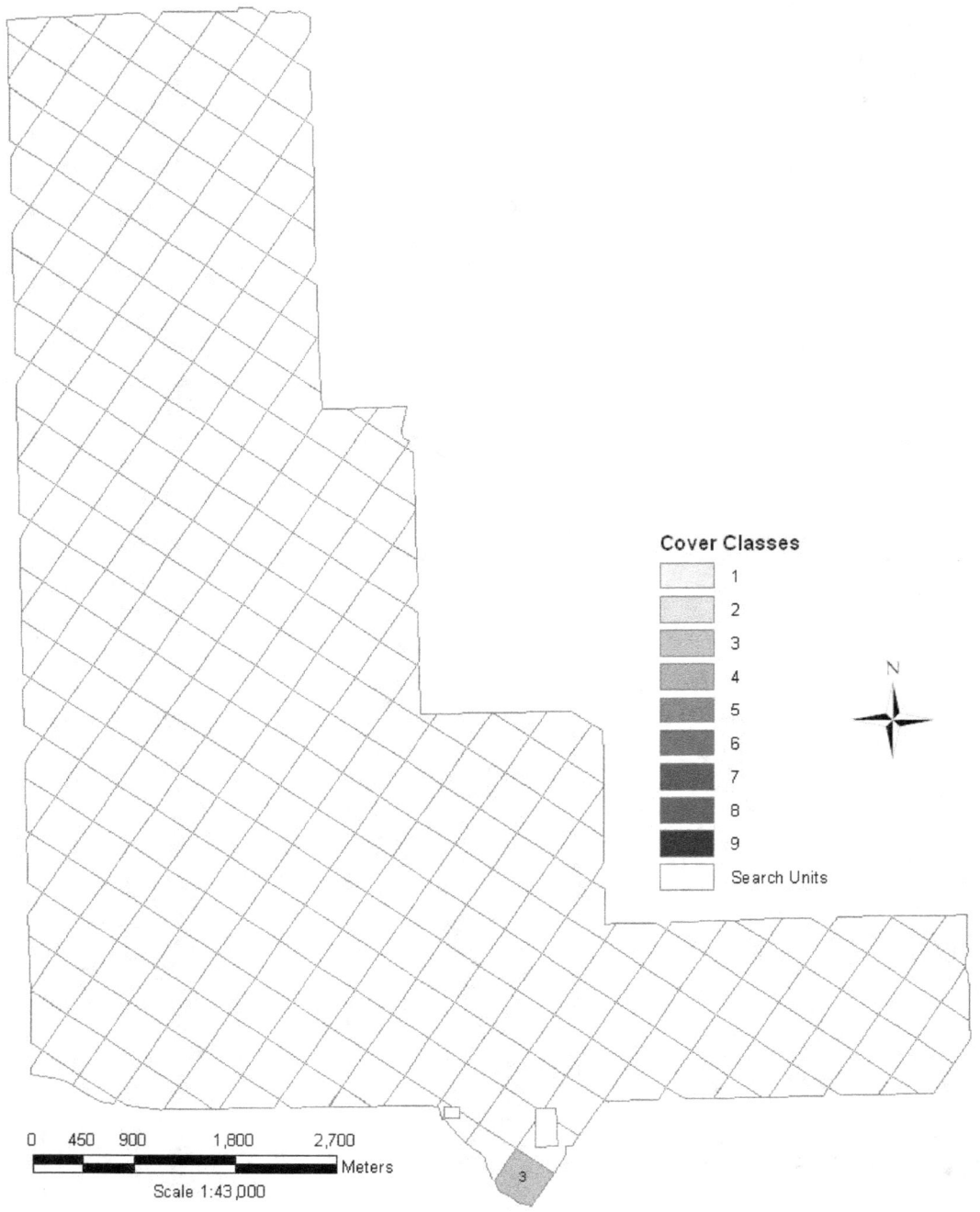

Figure 13. **Abundance and distribution of *Robinia pseudoacacia* (black locust) at Tallgrass Prairie National Preserve, 2006. Cover classes are as follows: 1=0.1-0.9 m^2, 2=1-9.9 m^2, 3=10-49.9 m^2, 4= 50-99.9 m^2, 5=100-499.9 m^2, 6= 499.9-999.9 m^2, 7=1,000-4,999.9 m^2, 8=5,000-9,999.9 m^2, and 9=10,000-14,999.9.**

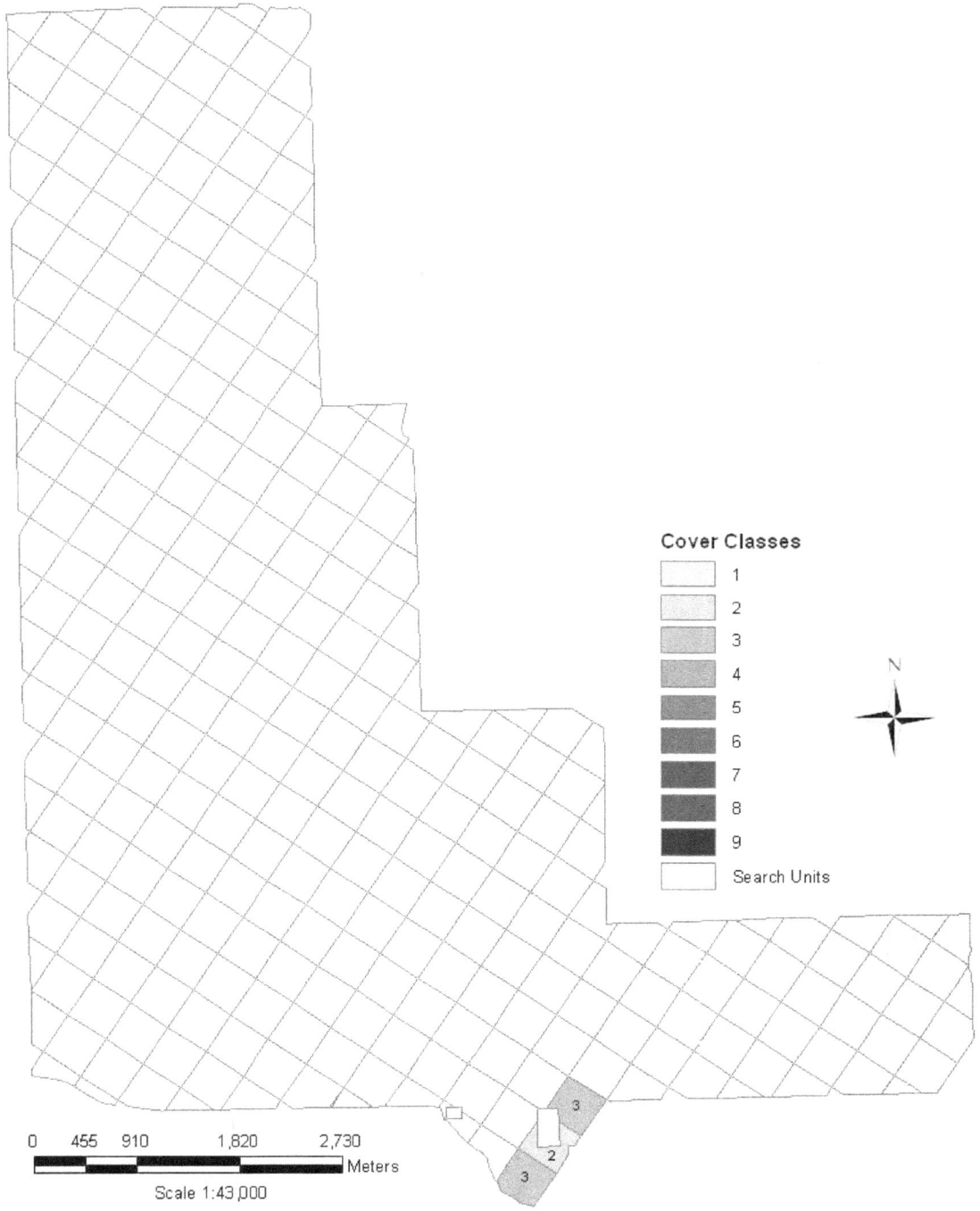

Figure 14. **Abundance and distribution of** *Scehdonorus* **spp (fescue) at Tallgrass Prairie National Preserve, 2006. Cover classes are as follows: 1=0.1-0.9 m^2, 2=1-9.9 m^2, 3=10-49.9 m^2, 4= 50-99.9 m^2, 5=100-499.9 m^2, 6= 499.9-999.9 m^2, 7=1,000-4,999.9 m^2, 8=5,000-9,999.9 m^2, and 9=10,000-14,999.9.**

Solanum rostratum - 2006

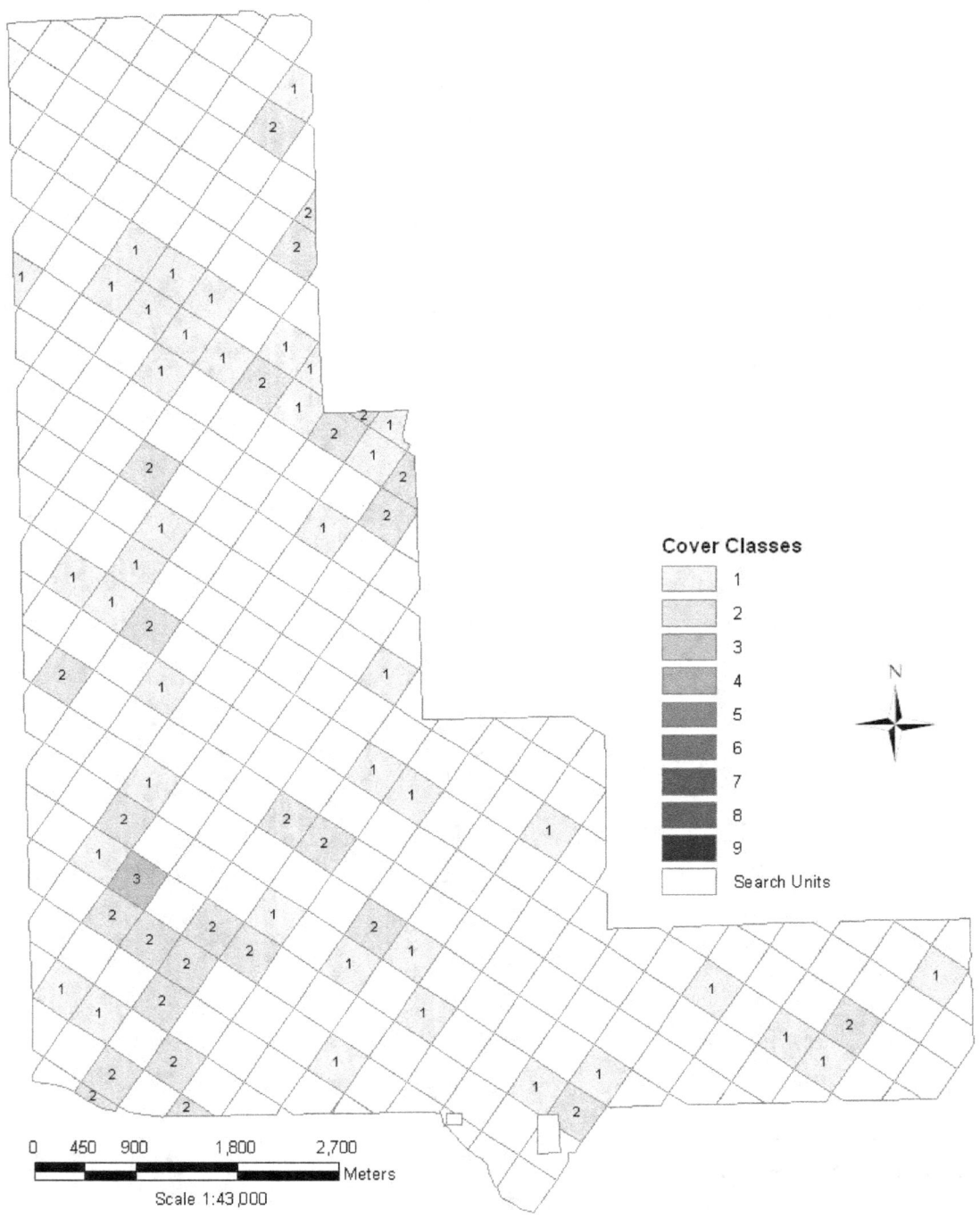

Figure 15. Abundance and distribution of *Solanum rostratum* (buffalo-bur nightshade) at Tallgrass Prairie National Preserve, 2006. Cover classes are as follows: 1=0.1-0.9 m², 2=1-9.9 m², 3=10-49.9 m², 4= 50-99.9 m², 5=100-499.9 m², 6= 499.9-999.9 m², 7=1,000-4,999.9 m², 8=5,000-9,999.9 m², and 9=10,000-14,999.9.

Sorghum halepense - 2006

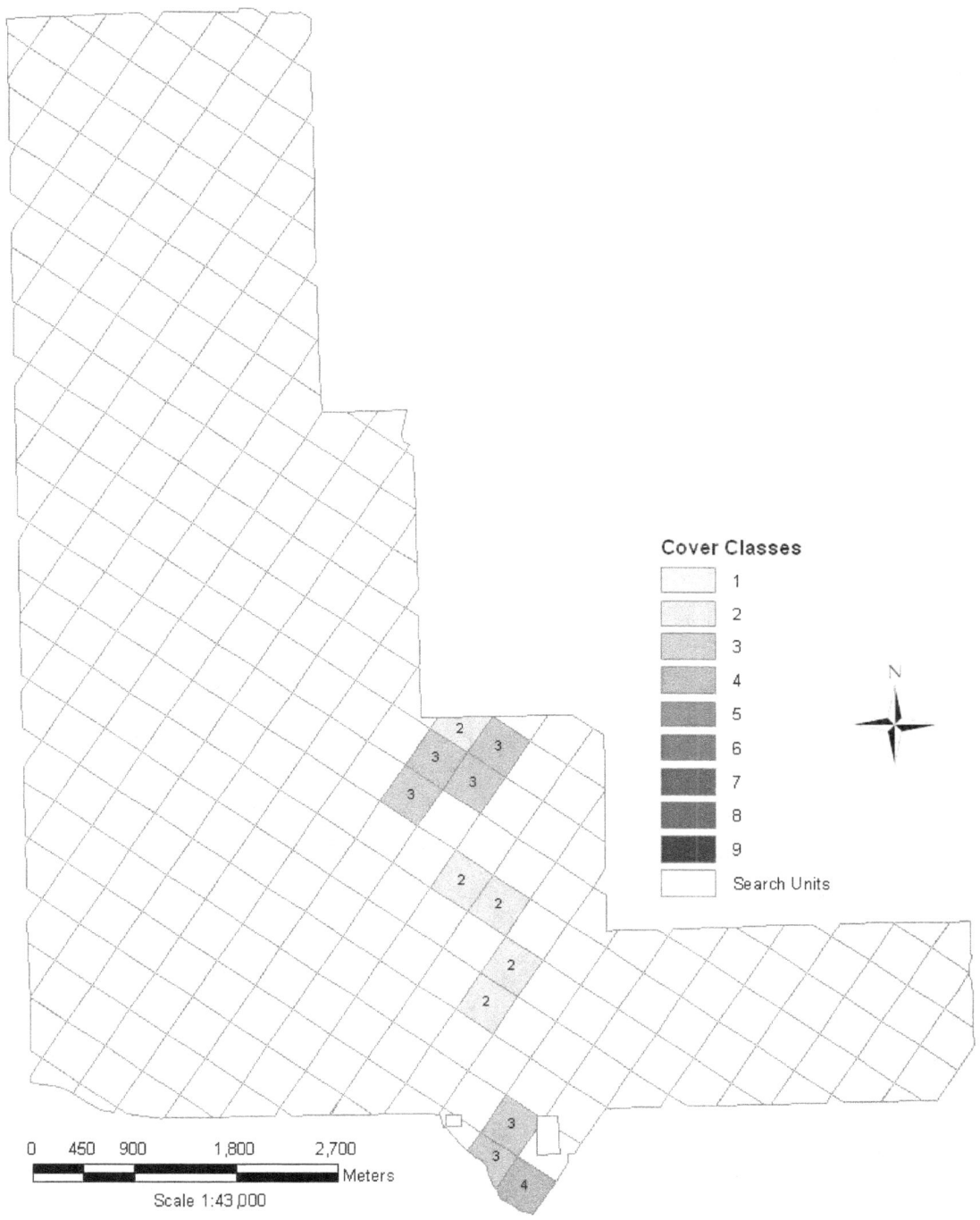

Figure 16. Abundance and distribution of *Sorghum halepense* (Johnsongrass) at Tallgrass Prairie National Preserve, 2006. Cover classes are as follows: 1=0.1-0.9 m^2, 2=1-9.9 m^2, 3=10-49.9 m^2, 4= 50-99.9 m^2, 5=100-499.9 m^2, 6= 499.9-999.9 m^2, 7=1,000-4,999.9 m^2, 8=5,000-9,999.9 m^2, and 9=10,000-14,999.9.

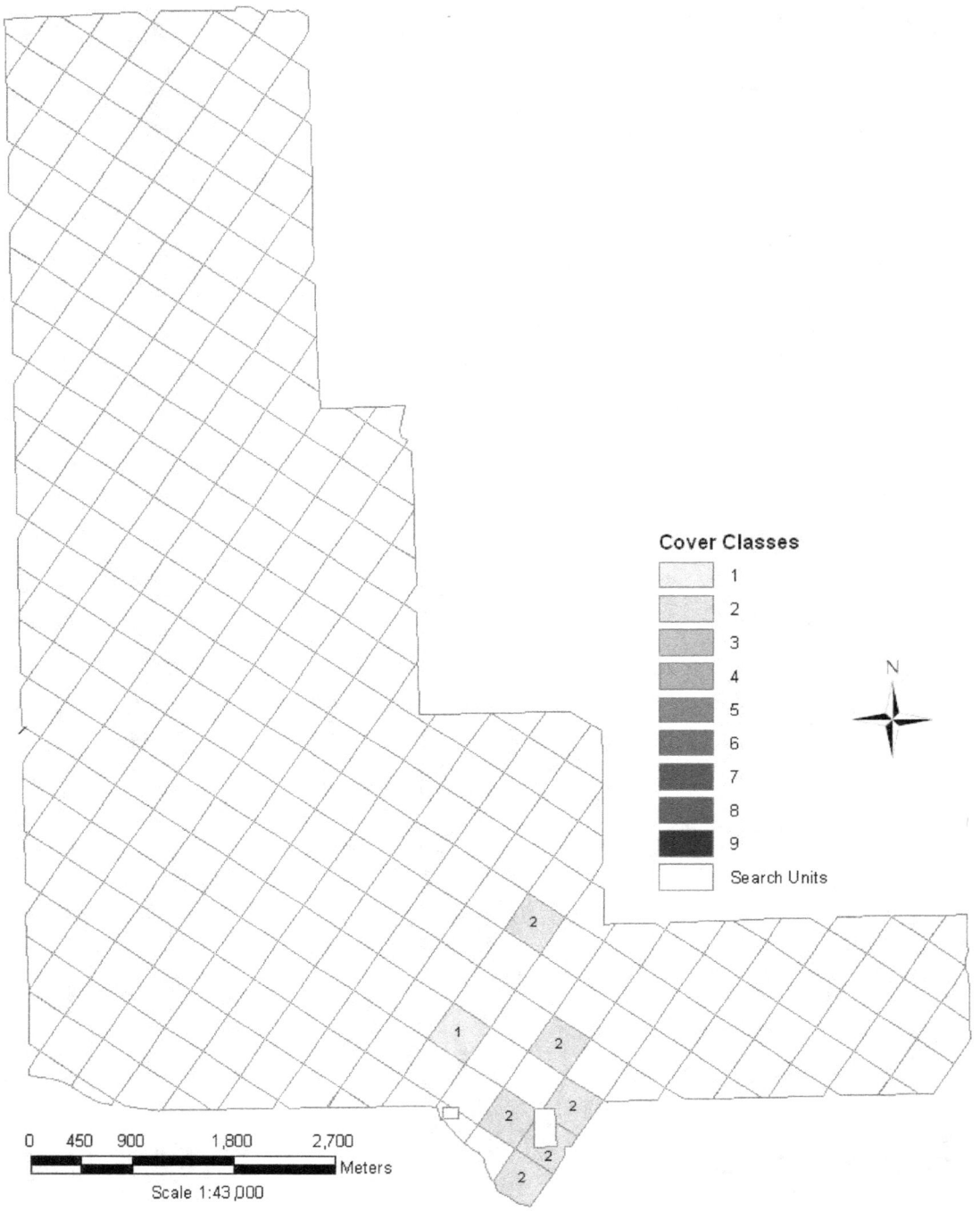

Figure 17. Abundance and distribution of *Torilis japonica* (Japanese hedge-parsley) at Tallgrass Prairie National Preserve, 2006. Cover classes are as follows: 1=0.1-0.9 m^2, 2=1-9.9 m^2, 3=10-49.9 m^2, 4= 50-99.9 m^2, 5=100-499.9 m^2, 6= 499.9-999.9 m^2, 7=1,000-4,999.9 m^2, 8=5,000-9,999.9 m^2, and 9=10,000-14,999.9.

Figure 18. Abundance and distribution of *Typha angustifolia* **(narrowleaf cattail) at Tallgrass Prairie National Preserve, 2006. Cover classes are as follows: 1=0.1-0.9 m², 2=1-9.9 m², 3=10-49.9 m², 4= 50-99.9 m², 5=100-499.9 m², 6= 499.9-999.9 m², 7=1000-4999.9 m², 8=5000-9999.9 m², and 9=10,000-14999.9.**

This page intentionally left blank.

The NPS has organized its parks with significant natural resources into 32 networks linked by geography and shared natural resource characteristics. HTLN is composed of 15 National Park Service (NPS) units in eight Midwestern states. These parks contain a wide variety of natural and cultural resources including sites focused on commemorating civil war battlefields, Native American heritage, westward expansion, and our U.S. Presidents. The Network is charged with creating inventories of its species and natural features as well as monitoring trends and issues in order to make sound management decisions. Critical inventories help park managers understand the natural resources in their care while monitoring programs help them understand meaningful change in natural systems and to respond accordingly. The Heartland Network helps to link natural and cultural resources by protecting the habitat of our history.

The I&M program bridges the gap between science and management with a third of its efforts aimed at making information accessible. Each network of parks, such as Heartland, has its own multi-disciplinary team of scientists, support personnel, and seasonal field technicians whose system of online databases and reports make information and research results available to all. Greater efficiency is achieved through shared staff and funding as these core groups of professionals augment work done by individual park staff. Through this type of integration and partnership, network parks are able to accomplish more than a single park could on its own.

The mission of the Heartland Network is to collaboratively develop and conduct scientifically credible inventories and long-term monitoring of park "vital signs" and to distribute this information for use by park staff, partners, and the public, thus enhancing understanding which leads to sound decision making in the preservation of natural resources and cultural history held in trust by the National Park Service.

www.nature.nps.gov/im/units/htln/

The U.S. Department of the Interior (DOI) is the nation's principal conservation agency, charged with the mission "*to protect and provide access to our Nation's natural and cultural heritage and honor our trust responsibilities to Indian tribes and our commitments to island communities.*" More specifically, Interior protects America's treasures for future generations, provides access to our nation's natural and cultural heritage, offers recreation opportunities, honors its trust responsibilities to American Indians and Alaska Natives and its responsibilities to island communities, conducts scientific research, provides wise stewardship of energy and mineral resources, fosters sound use of land and water resources, and conserves and protects fish and wildlife. The work that we do affects the lives of millions of people; from the family taking a vacation in one of our national parks to the children studying in one of our Indian schools.

NPS D-31, March 2007

Natural Resource Program Center
1201 Oakridge Drive, Suite 150
Fort Collins, CO 80525

www.nps.gov

EXPERIENCE YOUR AMERICA [T]

www.ingramcontent.com/pod-product-compliance
Lightning Source LLC
Chambersburg PA
CBHW080933290526
45795CB00007BA/2740